The Book of
Funk Beats
Grooves for Snare, Bass, and Hi-Hat

By David Lewitt

Cover art by Levin Pfeufer

Recording Credits: David Lewitt, Drums

Cherry Lane Music Company
Educational Director/Project Supervisor: Susan Poliniak
Director of Publications: Mark Phillips
Publications Coordinator: Rebecca Skidmore

ISBN 978-1-57560-922-5

Visit our website at www.cherrylaneprint.com

Table of Contents

Introduction

Welcome, Drummers!

This book is for intermediate to advanced players interested in improving their snare/bass technique and increasing their beat vocabulary. The grooves included are based on 12 patterns—some are classic funk patterns, others are less common—plus I have included exercises based on the samba beat. All of these patterns can help you to improve your technique and increase your beat vocabulary. When I wrote this book, my intention was to write every one of these beats so that they could be used in performance, either as a foundation groove or as a fill at the end of a phrase.

It is of the utmost importance to make these beats and solos flow evenly and musically. To get the most out of your practice, I suggest working through this book with a metronome so as to further develop your sense of meter and timing.

Always include the following in your practice regimen: rudiment work, reading (both on drumset and snare), and improvisation. Seek to expand and improve your playing by studying different styles and listening to other players.

Drumming is a vast art.

Practice hard and often.

How to Use This Book

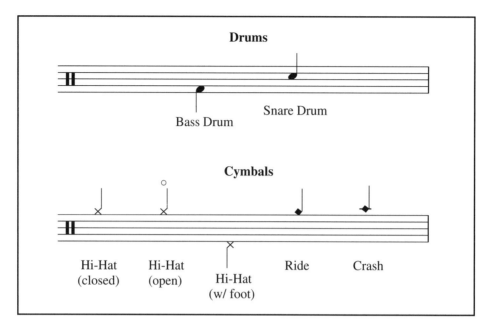

You will notice in the examples that the hi-hat (or cymbal) pattern is the basic eighth note rhythm.

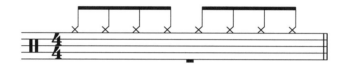

I encourage you, once you have mastered the grooves with straight eighth notes, to be creative with the hi-hat element. Feel free to embellish or simplify the part as desired.

Once you have mastered the beats as written, another change that you can try is to move the hi-hat hand to the cymbal and play the hi-hat with the foot in one of the following three patterns.

Play quarter notes on the beat.

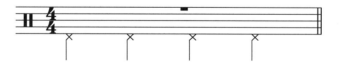

Play on just the "and" beats.

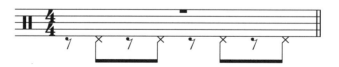

Play continuous eighth notes.

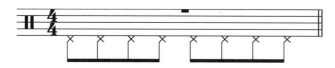

In a few places, I have indicated where you should open and close the hi-hat to create the classic "pea-soup" effect.

Cymbal embellishments you can play are listed below.

While playing the continuous eighth note pattern, accent the quarter note beats.

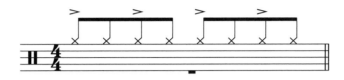

Play just quarter notes on the beat.

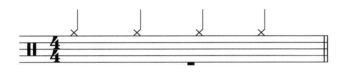

Play on just the "and" beats.

Here are some more difficult patterns you can try.

Play one eighth plus two 16ths per each quarter note beat.

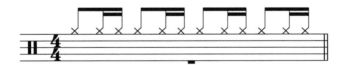

Play the reverse of the above pattern.

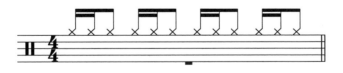

Play continuous 16th notes. Slow it down for this one-handed pattern. The right or left hand can lead.

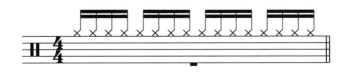

You can also play through this entire book using your weak hand as your cymbal/hi-hat hand.

This book is formatted so that you can easily glue two measures together by simply reading across the line, thereby forming a two-bar pattern. For instance, you can take patterns 479 and 480 and put them together to make a nice two-bar phrase.

You can also take the pattern on the left side of the page, play it three times, and then play the pattern on the right side to create a nice four-bar phrase. Take patterns 1 and 2, for example.

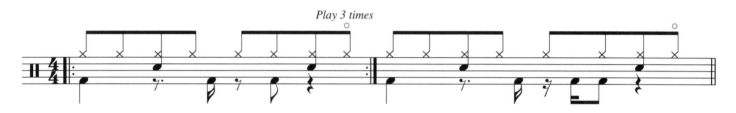

You can also play each page straight thru, creating a little beat study or drum étude.

However you choose to play, the most important thing is to make the patterns "groove." It is more important to master one beat and *really* make it work rather than to play through a whole page in a half-baked manner. Groove and flow are paramount—quality over quantity, in other words.

A Word About Tempo

Most of this book should be played in the range of 80 to 120 beats per minute, but no matter what tempo you are using, always be musical. Listen to what you are playing. Is it grooving? Does the beat flow? Are you able to execute all of the notes clearly and cleanly? Is the tempo that you are using "working" for that beat? Try to listen to yourself as a "third-party"—in other words, be objective about what you are doing.

Note: CD tracks begin with the *Solos* section on page 58.

About the Author

Dave Lewitt was born on Long Island, New York, and grew up musically during the fusion era of the early 1970s. He started playing clubs at the age of 15 with a variety of bands, and during his college years toured the eastern United States extensively and shared the stage with a number of artists, including Humble Pie, Foghat, Leon Redbone, The Joe Perry Project, and the Tubes. In 1983, he received his BFA from the Conservatory of Music at Purchase College, State University of New York. After college he toured with Maria Muldaur in *The Pirates of Penzance*, and started his own funk-reggae band, Redstripe, which eventually became Banzai Pipeline. With his band, he toured the Northeast and college circuit for ten years playing hundreds of shows, and produced five CDs. In Banzai/Redstripe's time together, they warmed up for many artists, including Jimmy Cliff, The Wailers, Black Uhuru, Yellowman, and the Meditations.

Dave has also done extensive work with Mark Wood, including playing with The Trans-Siberian Orchestra, the Mark Wood Band (as well as tours to Europe, Canada, and the US), and on his two Guitar Recordings releases: *Voodoo Violince* and *Against the Grain*.

Dave has worked for the Conservatory of Dance at Purchase College as a staff musician and composer since 1983. He has composed a number of pieces for modern dance that have been performed at venues including Avery Fisher Hall, the Joyce Theater, Dance Theatre Workshop, and the Performing Arts Center at Purchase College. He also teaches hand drumming at Purchase, and has been teaching drums for the past 25 years in the New York area.

Photo by Wayne Dennon

Dave's recording credits include:

CBS: *Sports Spectacular* Theme; 1992 Olympics; Coverage of the Tour De France in 2001, 2002 (Emmy for Best Sports Score), 2003, 2004, 2005, and 2006
ESPN *SportsCenter:* music for football, hockey and baseball highlights
Mark Wood: *Voodoo Violince* (1995), *Against the Grain* (1997), *Guts, Grace, and Glory* (2000), *These Are a Few of My Favorite Things* (2001), *Portrait of an Artist* (2003)
Dave Pettigrew—*Teach Me How to Fly* (2004)
Neil Alexander—*Alone at Last* (2001)

Acknowledgments

Special thanks to the Lewitt family, Celine Pittet, Richie Morales, John Stix, Tommy De Martino, Susan Poliniak, Marshall Woodall, Jerry Korobow, Al Pollick, George Nolte, Ray DesRoches, Dick Horowitz, Narada Michael Walden, Kenwood Dennard, the Nail, Larry B, Karson H., and Miles D.

Grooves

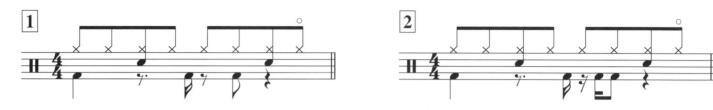

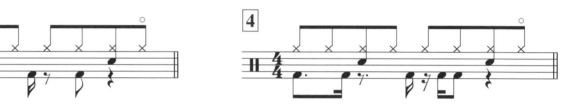

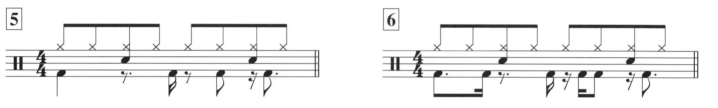

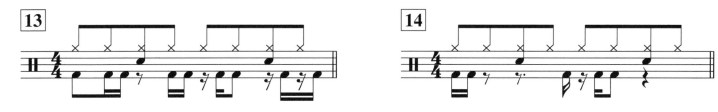

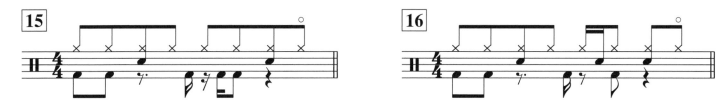

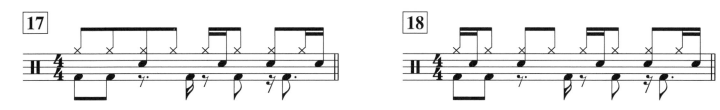

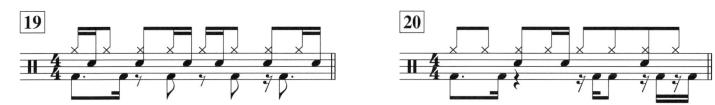

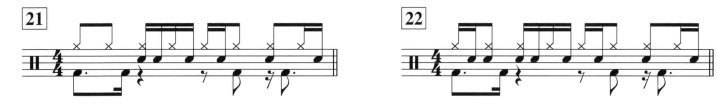

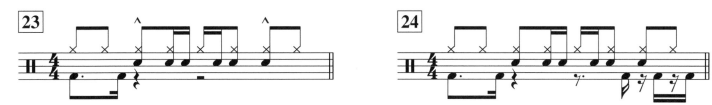

25

26

27
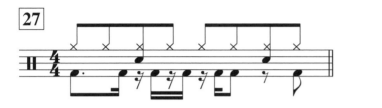

28

29
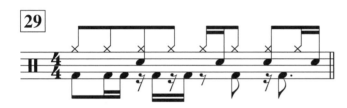

30
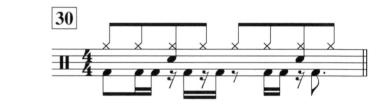

31

32
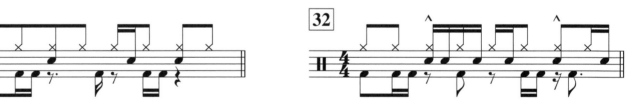

33

34

35

36

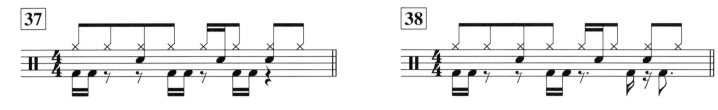

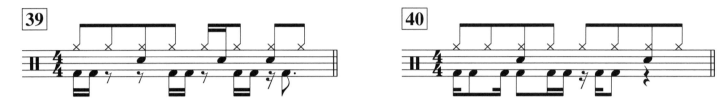

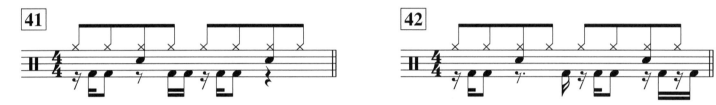

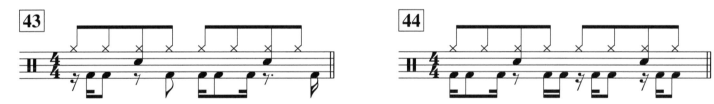

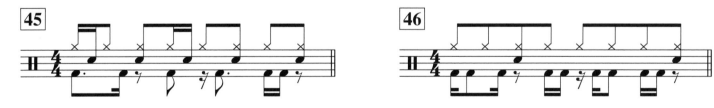

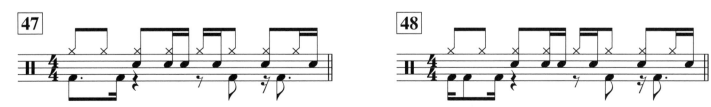

Grooves *cont.*

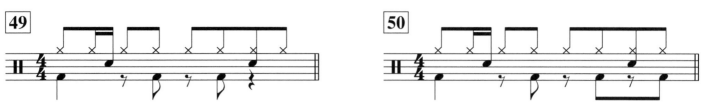

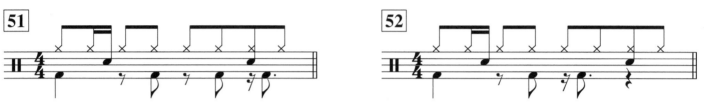

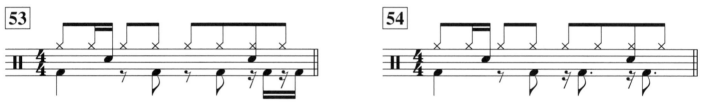

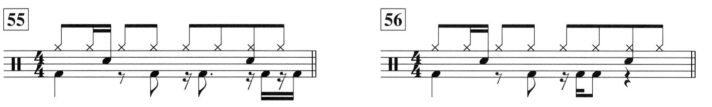

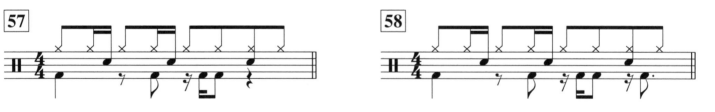

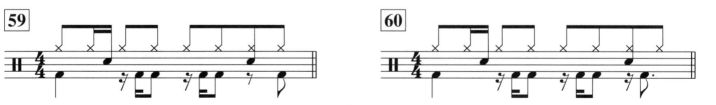

61

62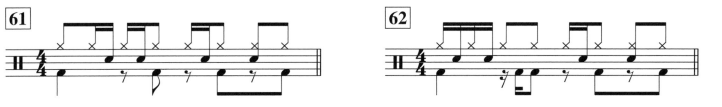

63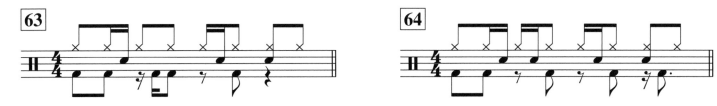

64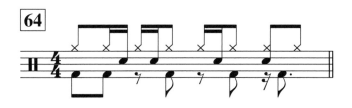

65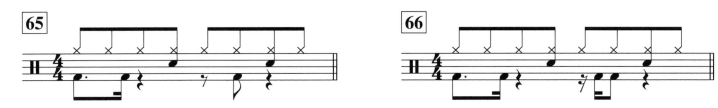

66

67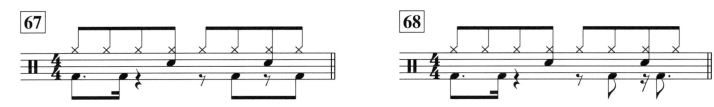

68

69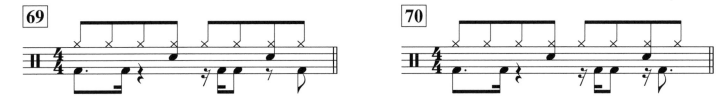

70

71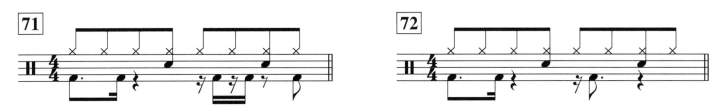

72

Grooves *cont.*

73

74

75

76
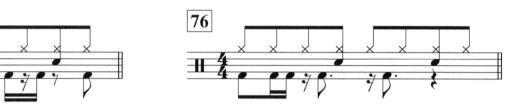

77

78

79

80
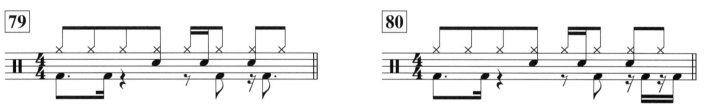

81

82
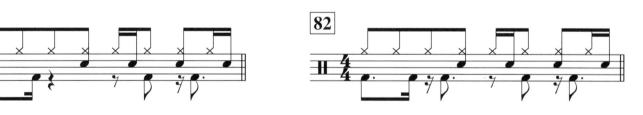

83
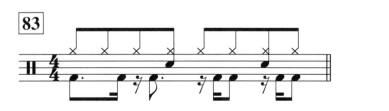

84

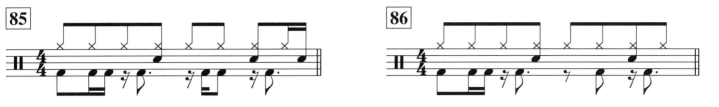

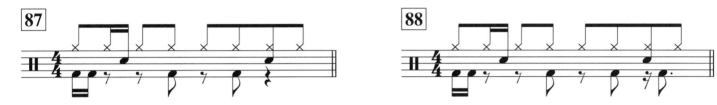

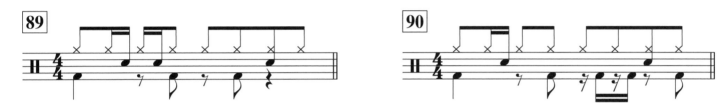

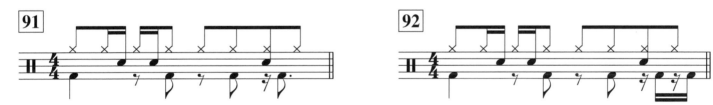
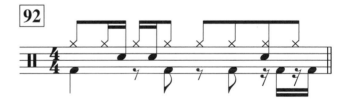

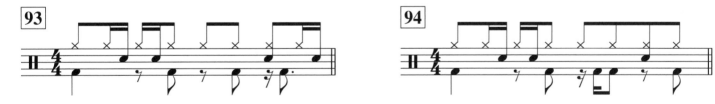

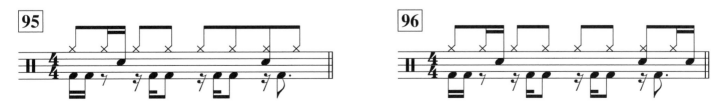

97

98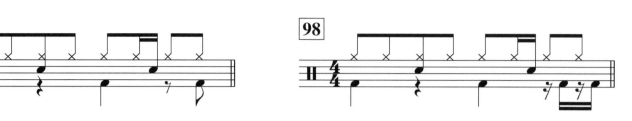

99

100

101

102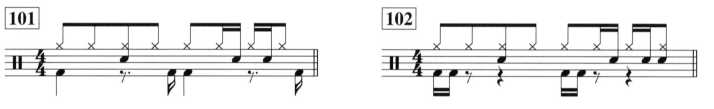

103

104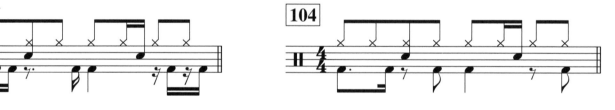

105

106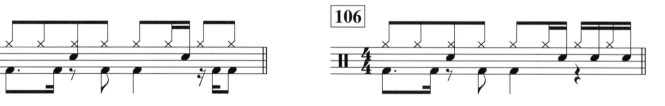

107

108

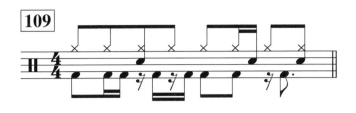

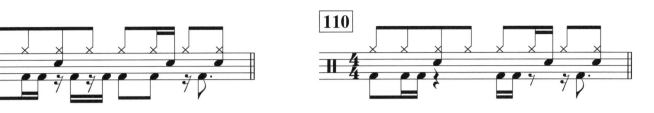

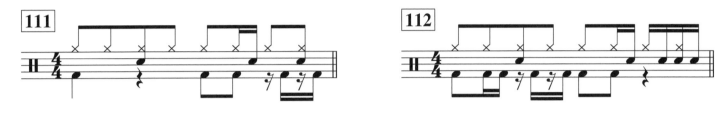

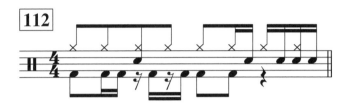

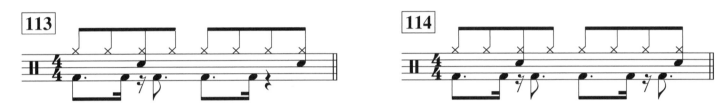

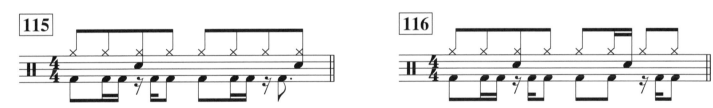

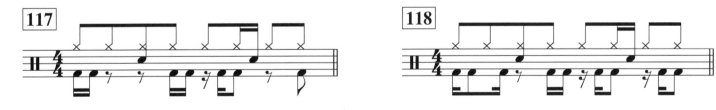

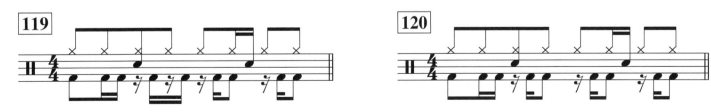

121

122

123

124

125

126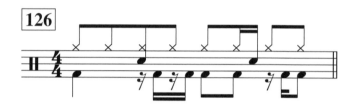

127

128

129

130

131

132

133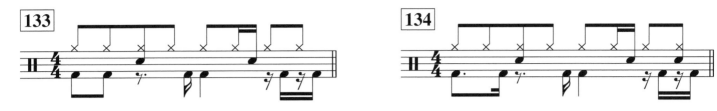

134

135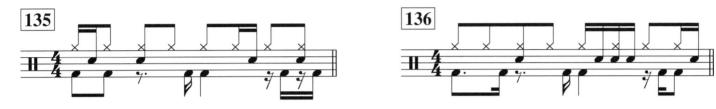

136

137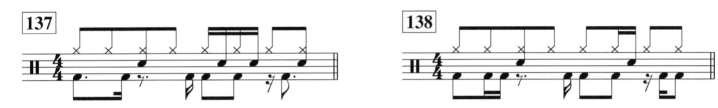

138

139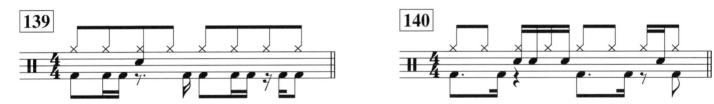

140

141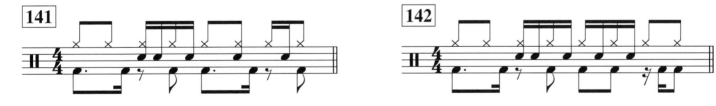

142

143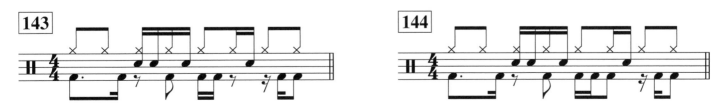

144

145

146

147

148

149

150

151

152

153

154

155

156

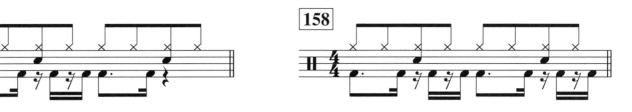

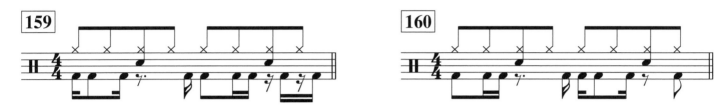

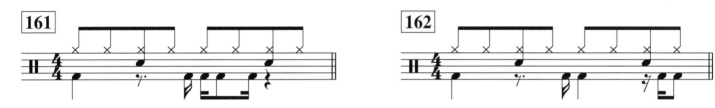

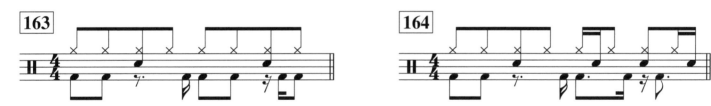

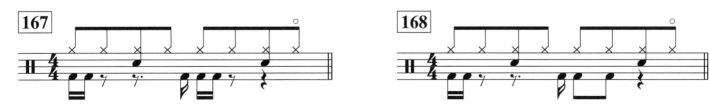

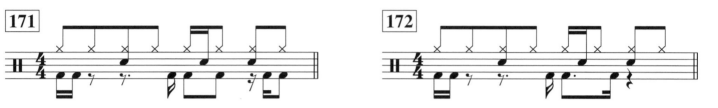

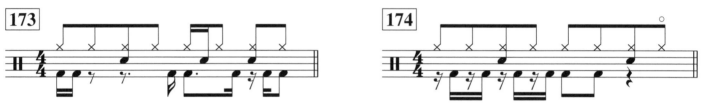

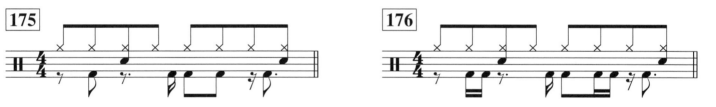

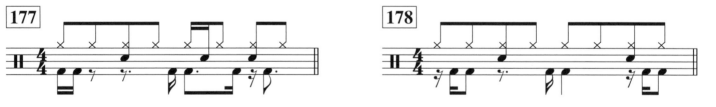

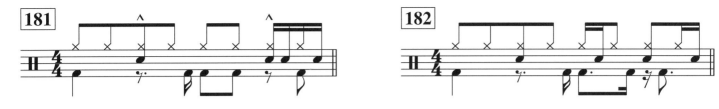

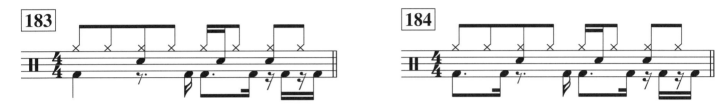

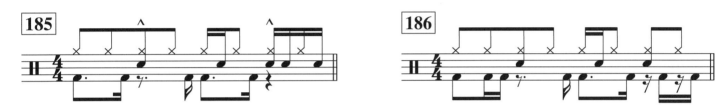

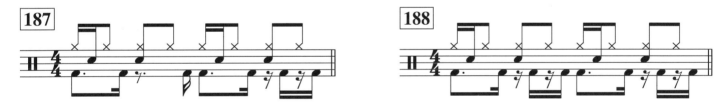

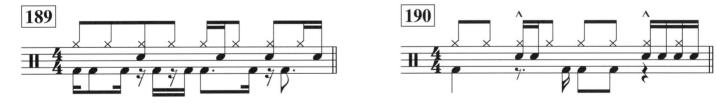

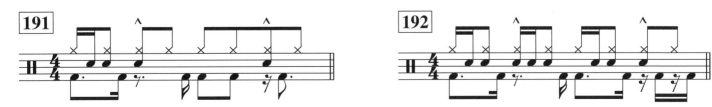

193

194

195

196

197

198

199

200

201
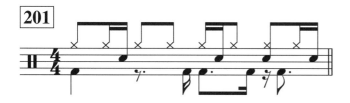

202

203

204

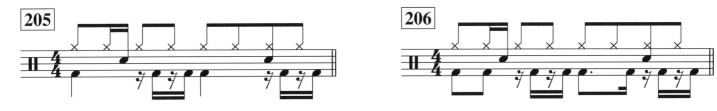

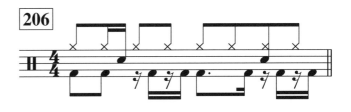

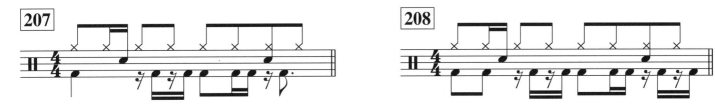

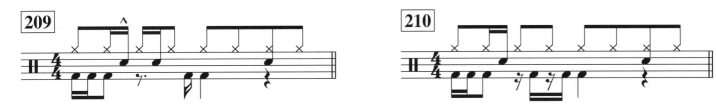

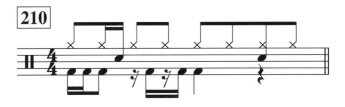

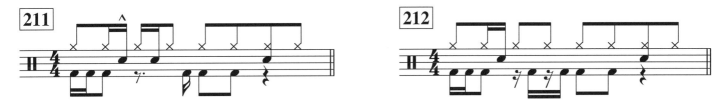

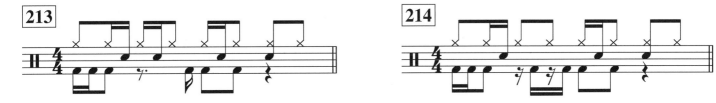

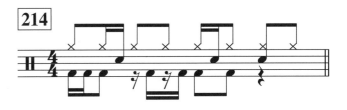

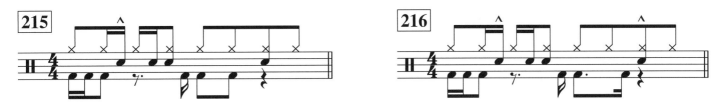

217

218

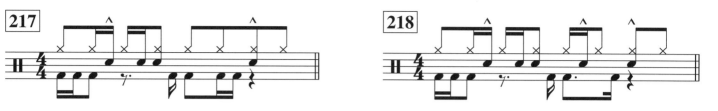

219

220

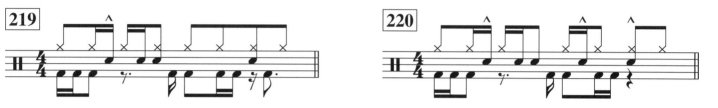

221

222

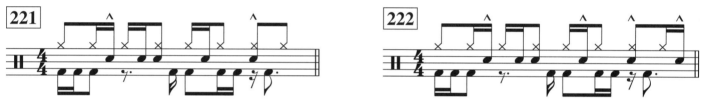

223

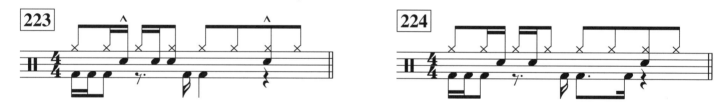

224

225

226

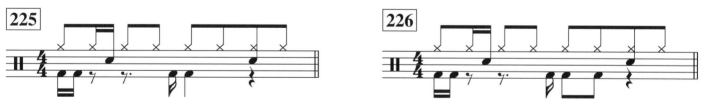

227

228

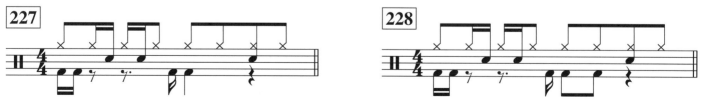

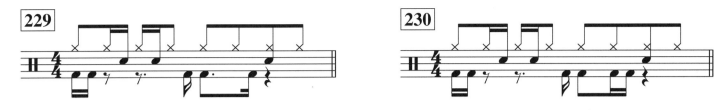

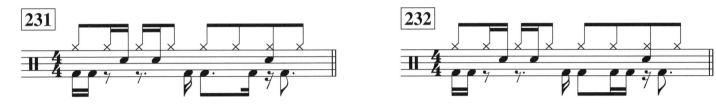

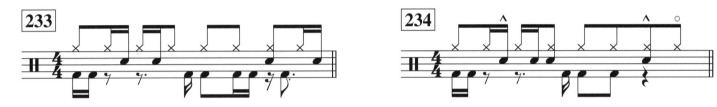

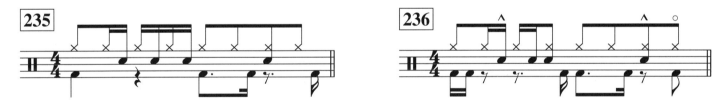

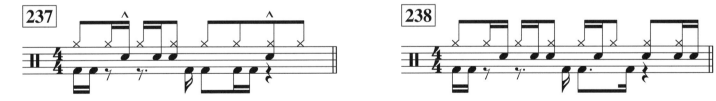

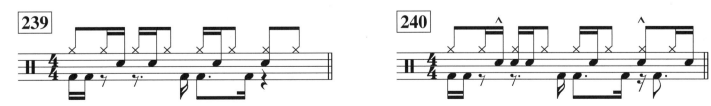

241

242

243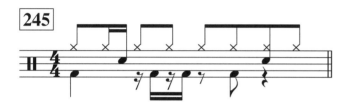

244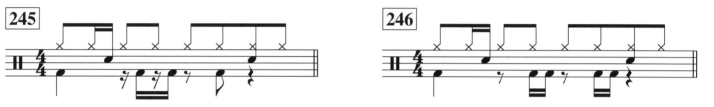

245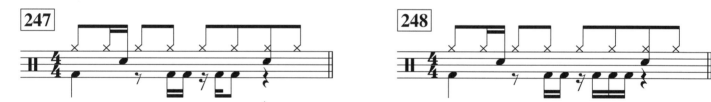

246

247

248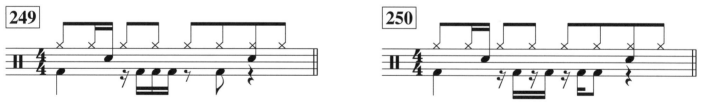

249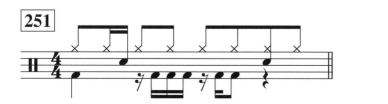

250

251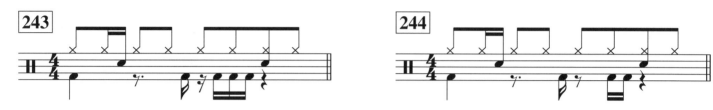

252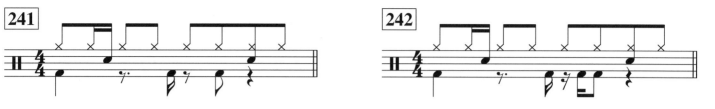

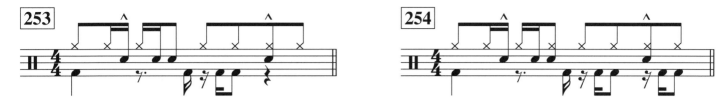

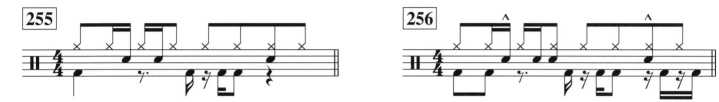

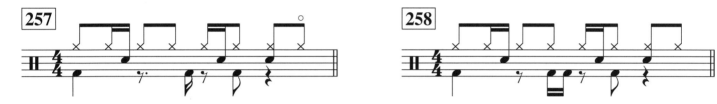

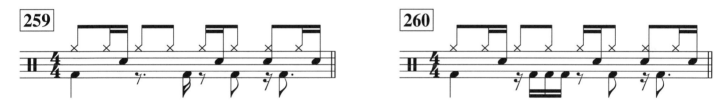

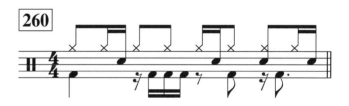

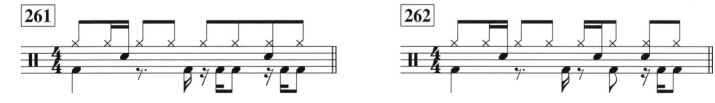

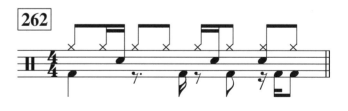

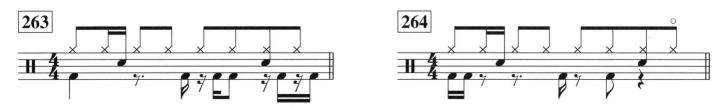

Grooves *cont.*

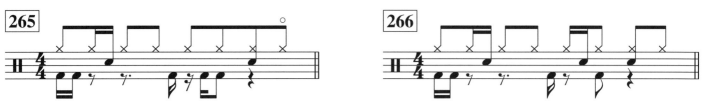

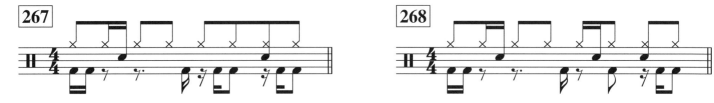

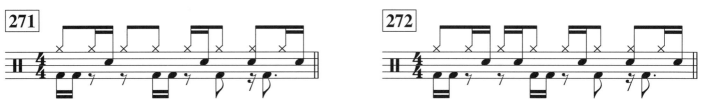

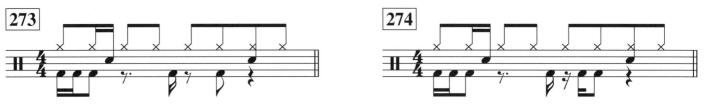

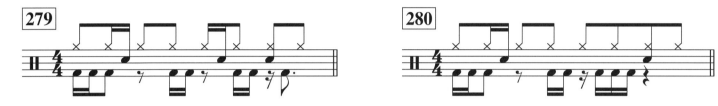

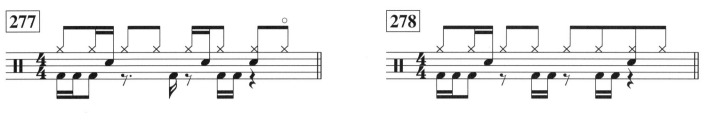

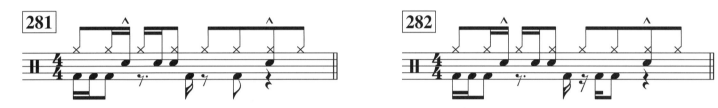

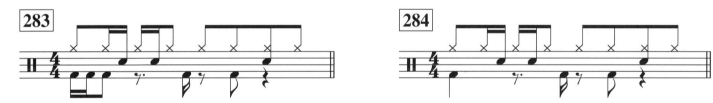

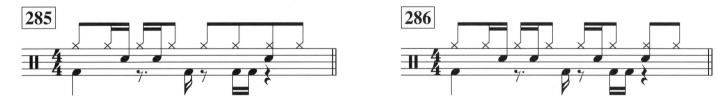

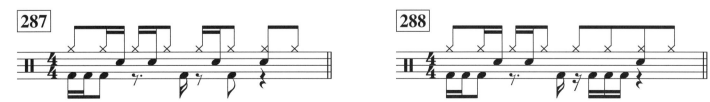

289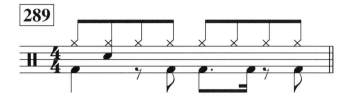

290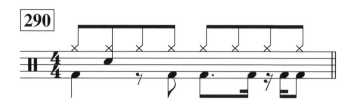

291

292

293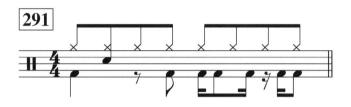

294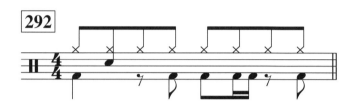

295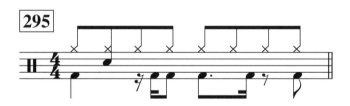

296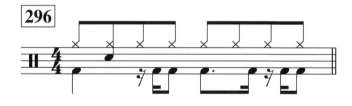

297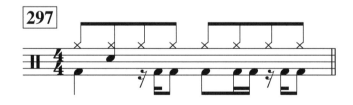

298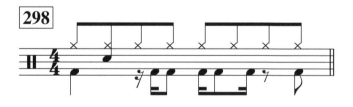

299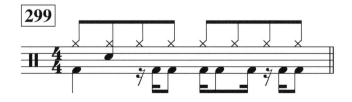

300

301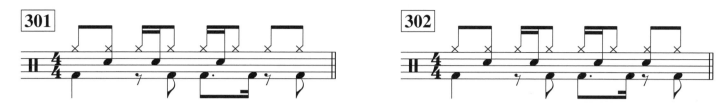

302

303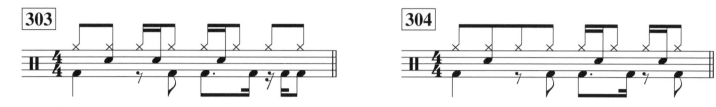

304

305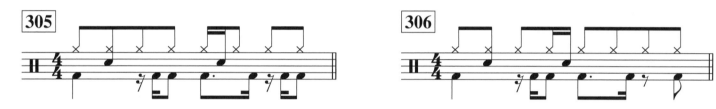

306

307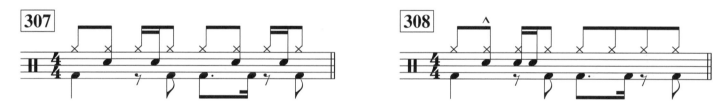

308

309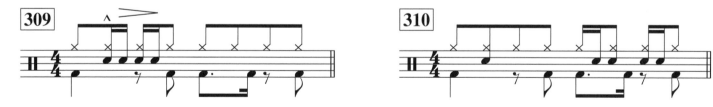

310

311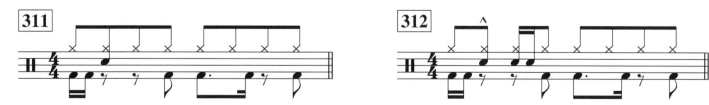

312

313

314
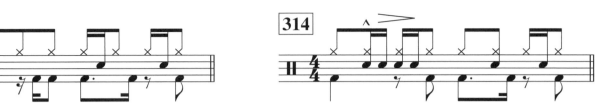

315
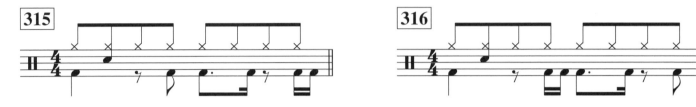

316
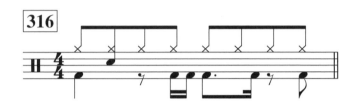

317

318
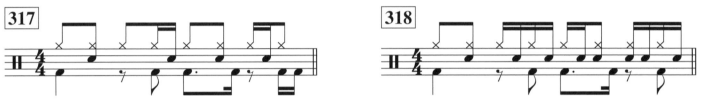

319

320

321

322
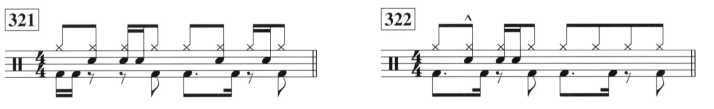

323

324

325

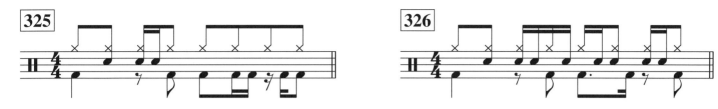

326

327

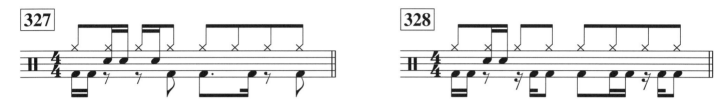

328

329

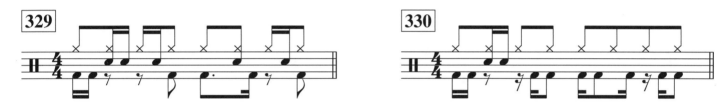

330

331

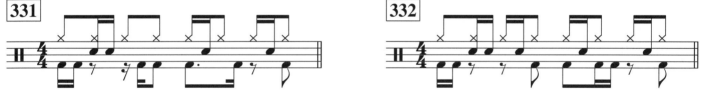

332

333

334

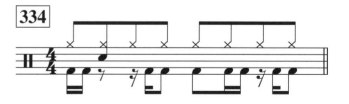

335

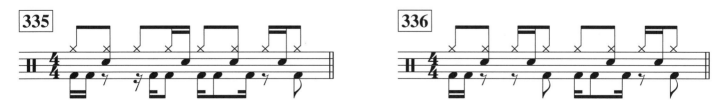

336

337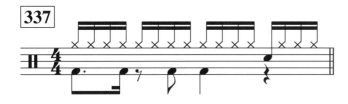

338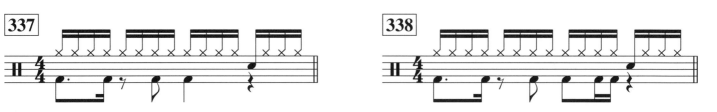

339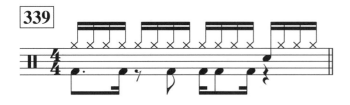

340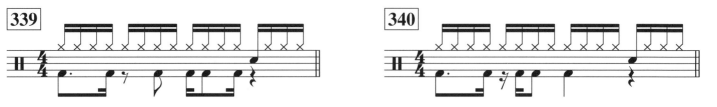

341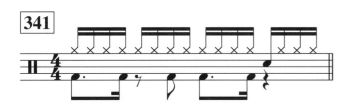

342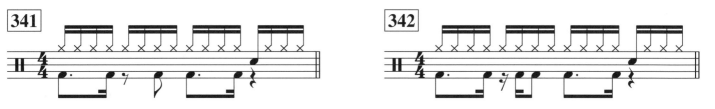

343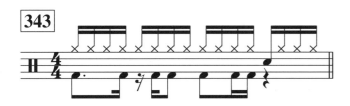

344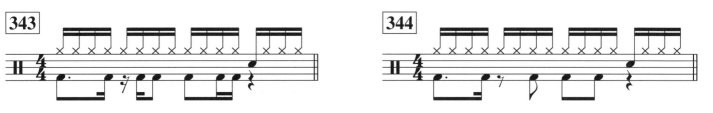

345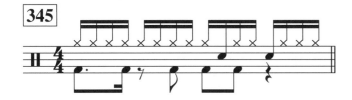

346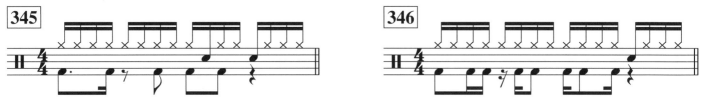

347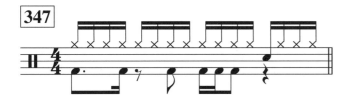

348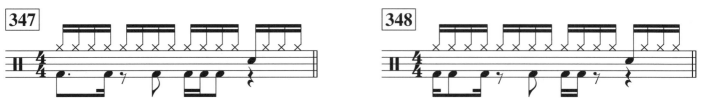

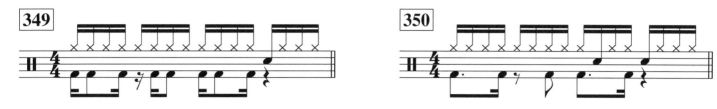

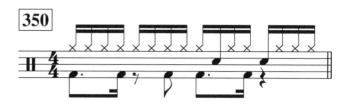

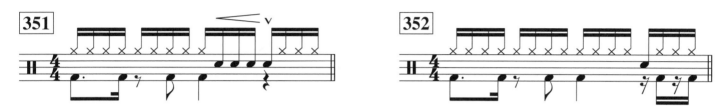

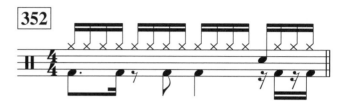

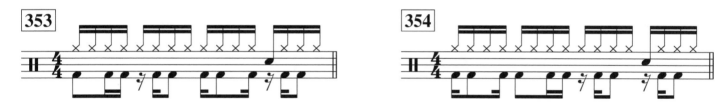

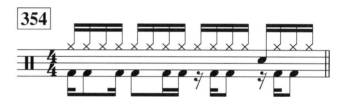

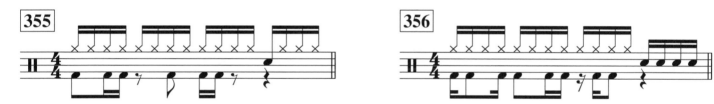

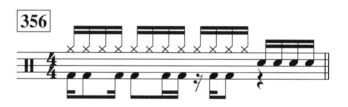

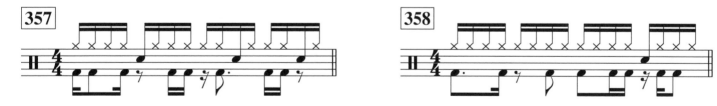

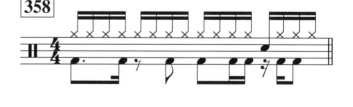

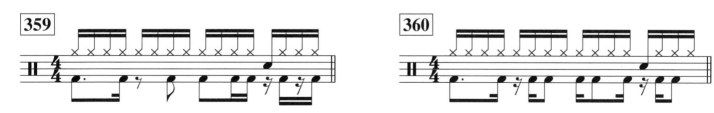

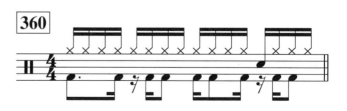

361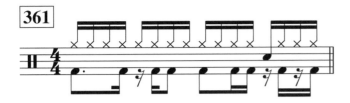

362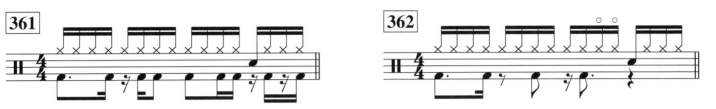

363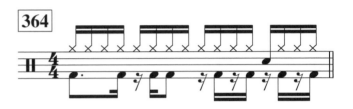

364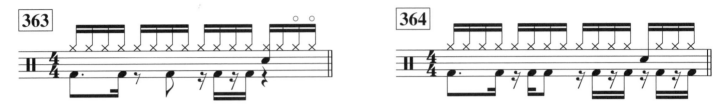

365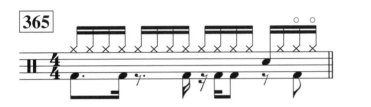

366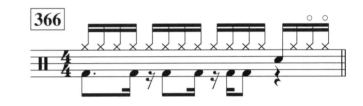

367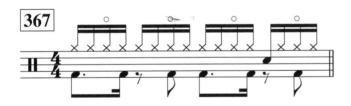

368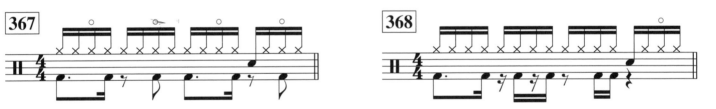

369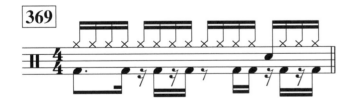

370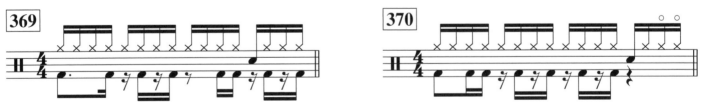

371

372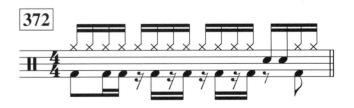

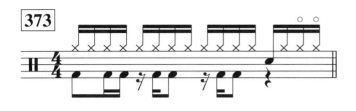

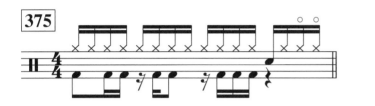

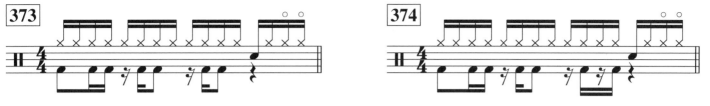

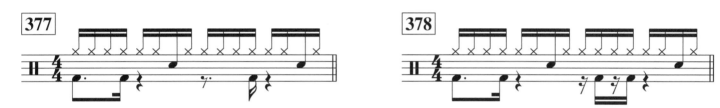

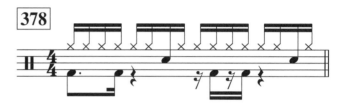

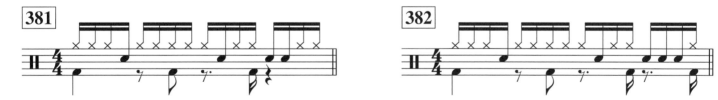

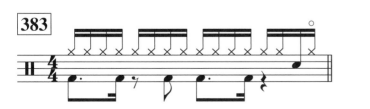

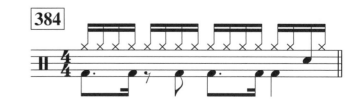

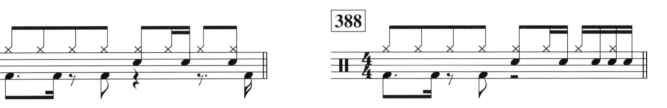

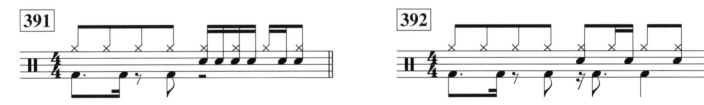

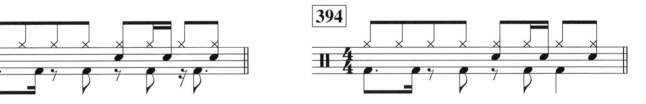

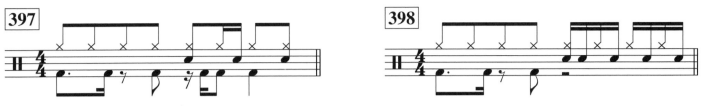

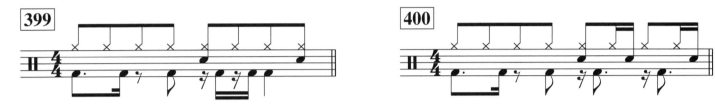

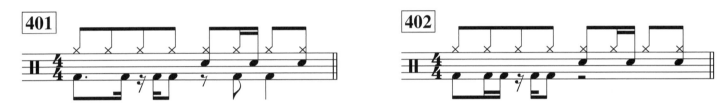

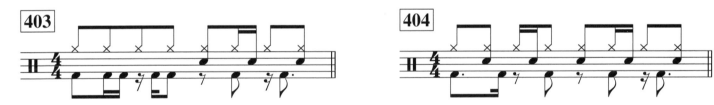

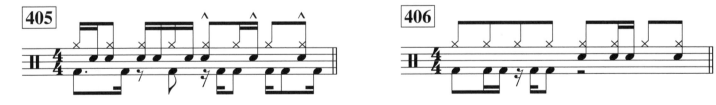

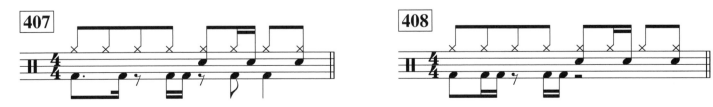

409

410

411

412
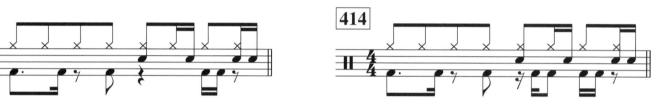

413
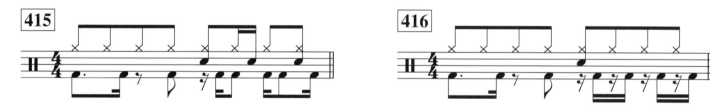
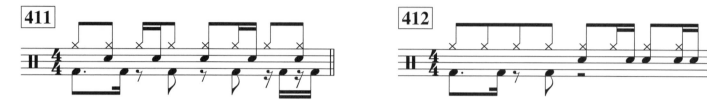

414

415

416

417

418
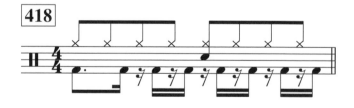

419
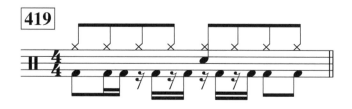

420

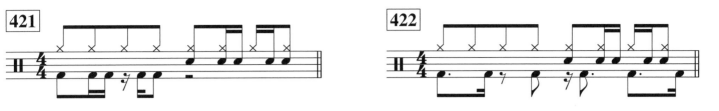

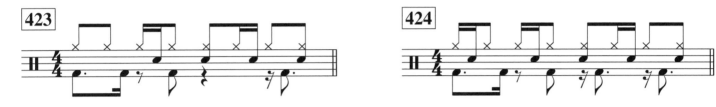

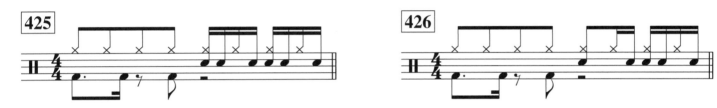

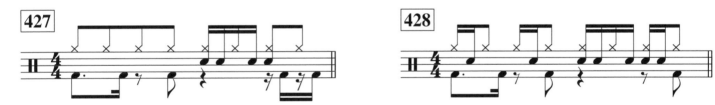

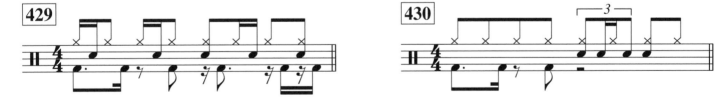

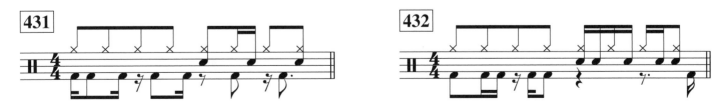

433

434
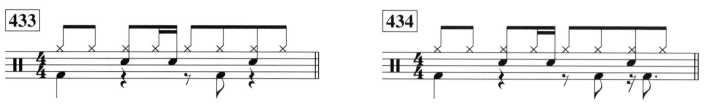

435

436
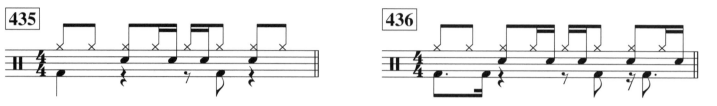

437

438
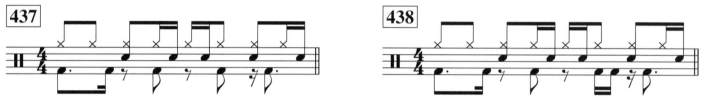

439

440
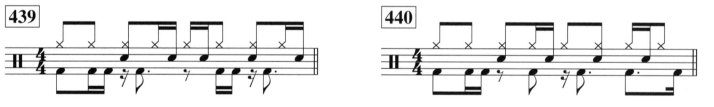

441

442
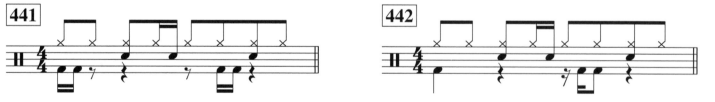

443

444
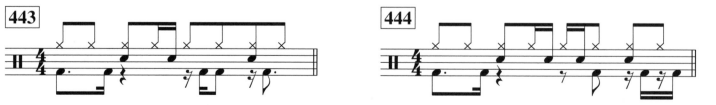

445

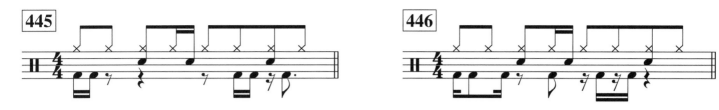

446

447

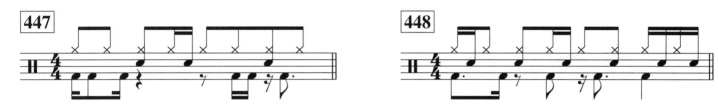

448

449

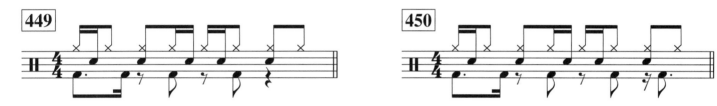

450

451

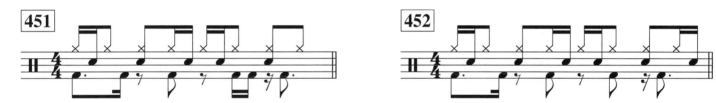

452

453

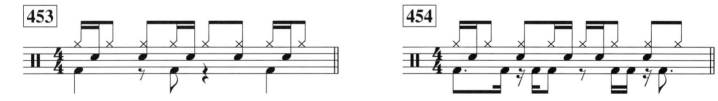

454

455

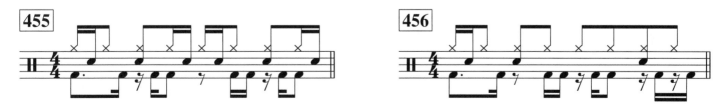

456

Grooves *cont.*

457

458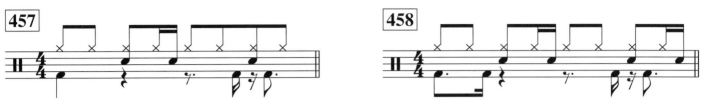

459

460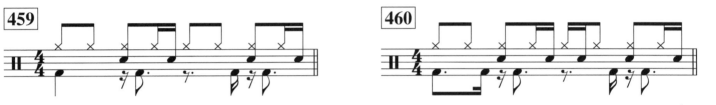

461

462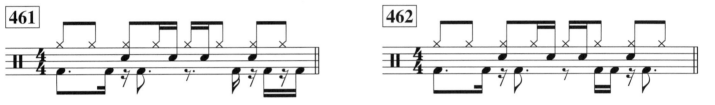

463

464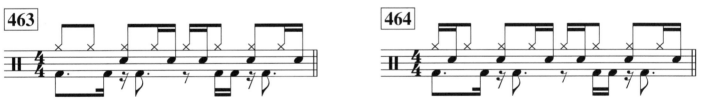

465

466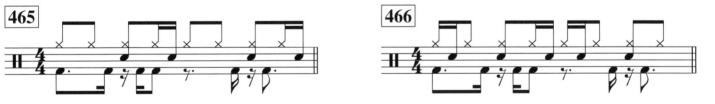

467

468

469

470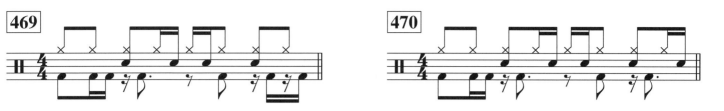

471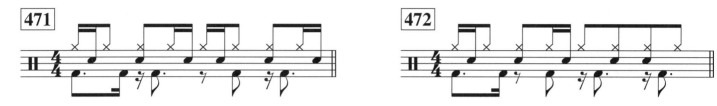

472

473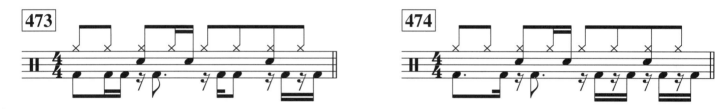

474

475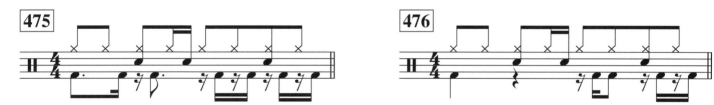

476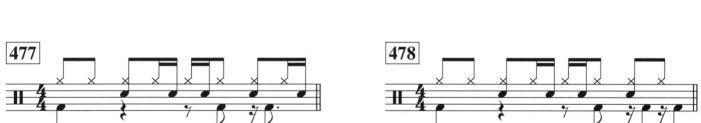

477

478

479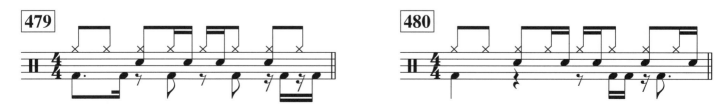

480

481
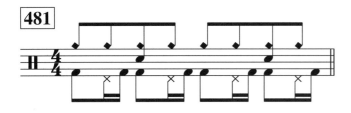

482
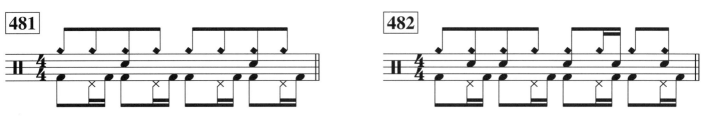

483
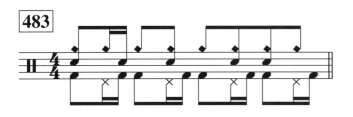

484
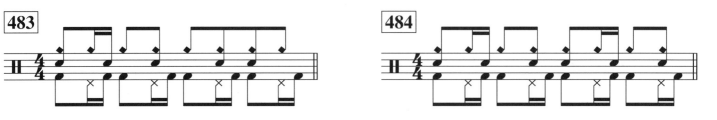

485
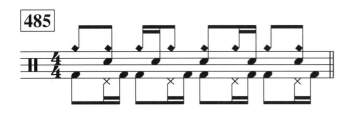

486
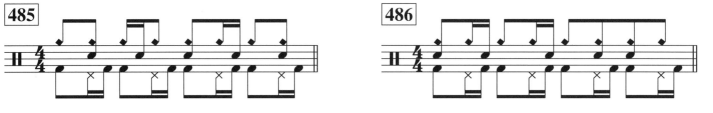

487
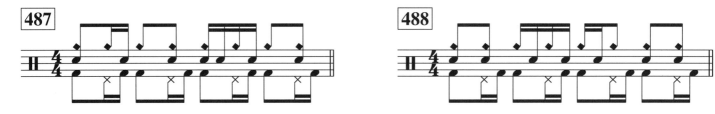

488

489
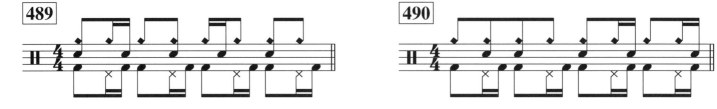

490
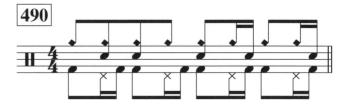

491
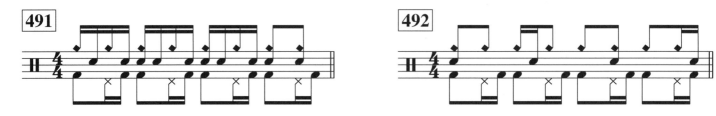

492
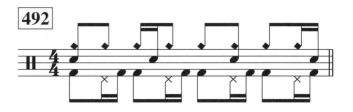

493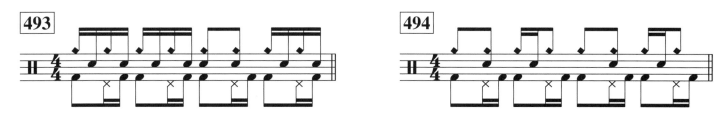

494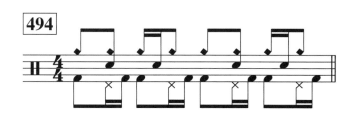

495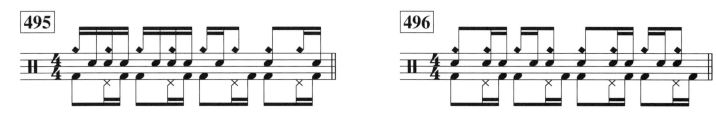

496

497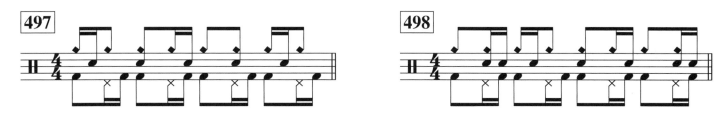

498

499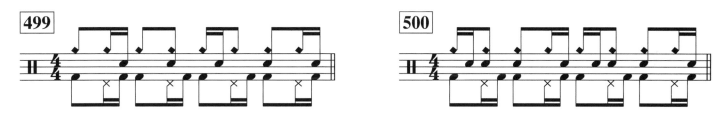

500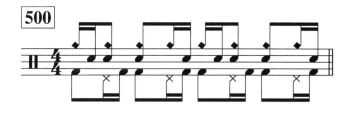

501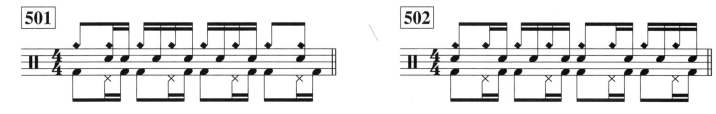

502

503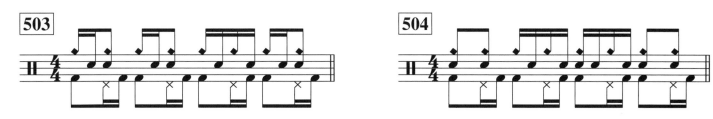

504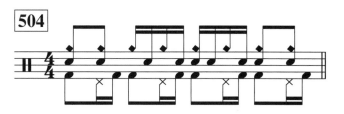

505

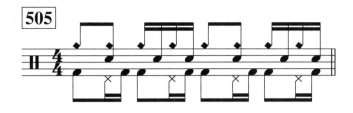

506

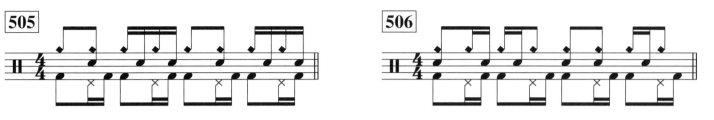

507

508

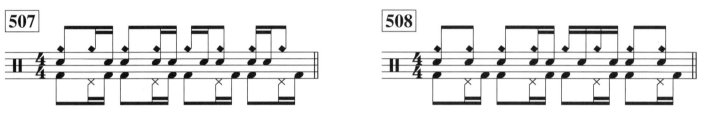

509

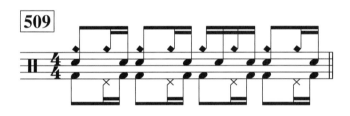

510

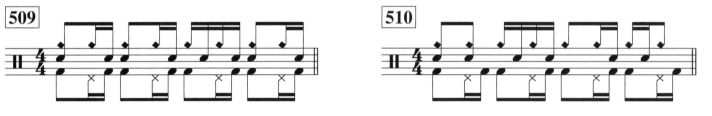

511

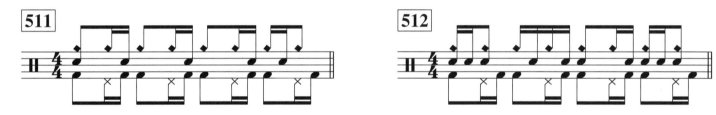

512

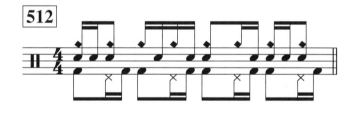

513

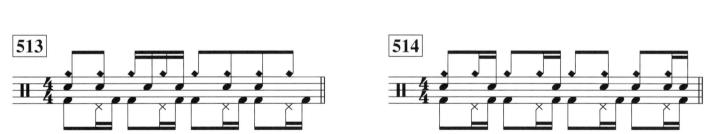

514

515

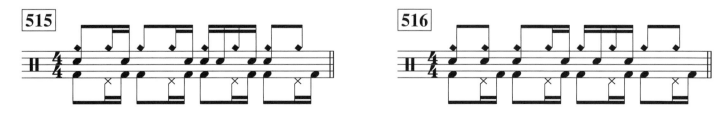

516

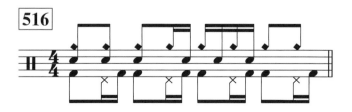

517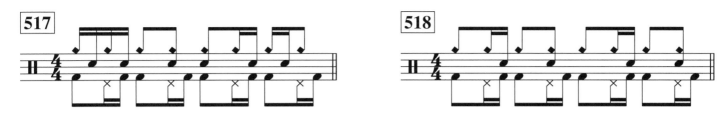

518

519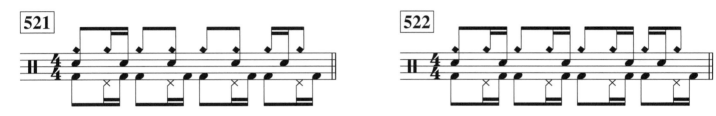

520

521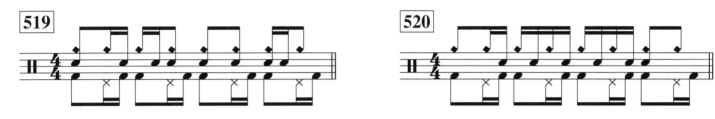

522

523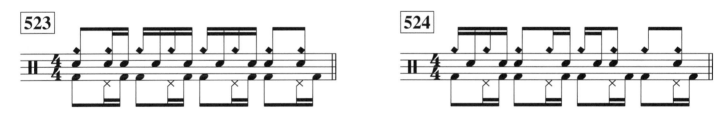

524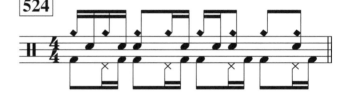

525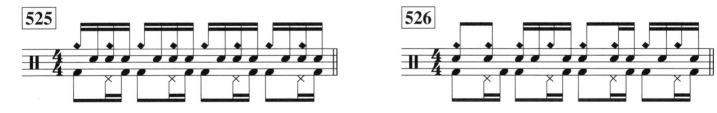

526

527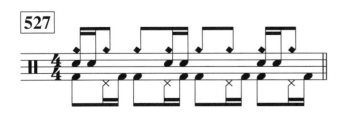

528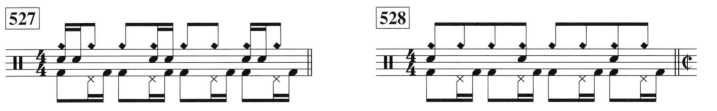

529

530

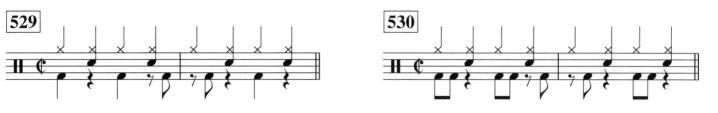

531

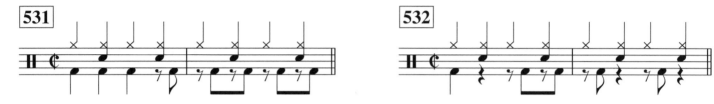

532

533

534

535

536

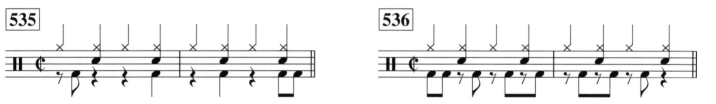

537

538

539

540

541

542

543

544

545

546

547

548

549

550

551

552

553

554

555

556

557
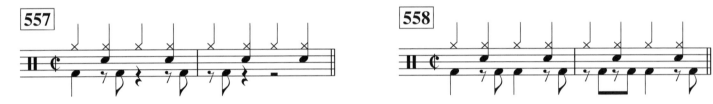

558

559

560

561

562
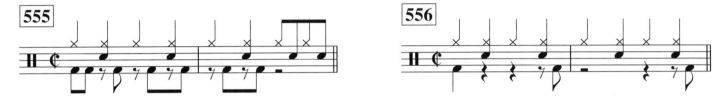

563

564
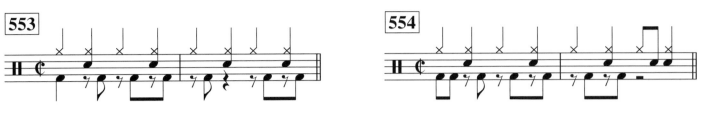

565

566

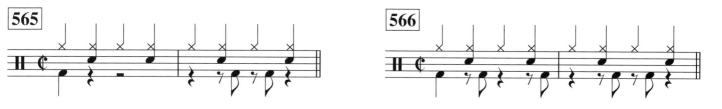

567

568

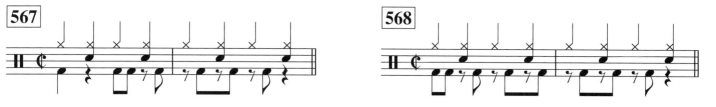

569

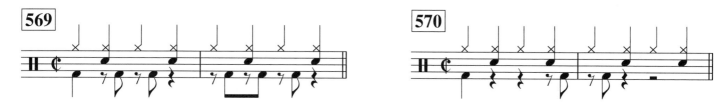

570

571

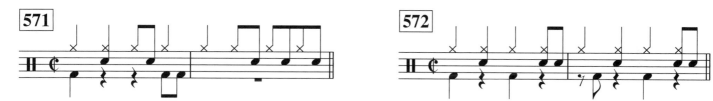

572

573

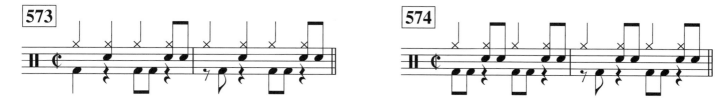

574

575

576

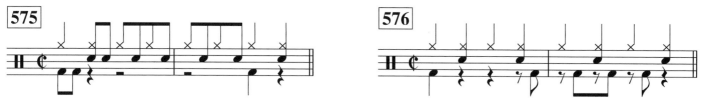

577

578

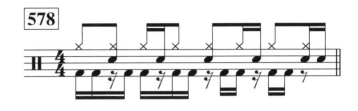

579

580

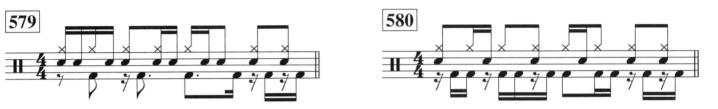

581

582

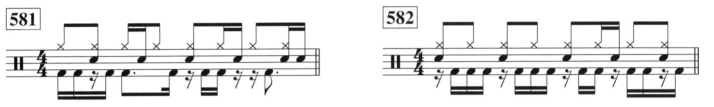

583

584

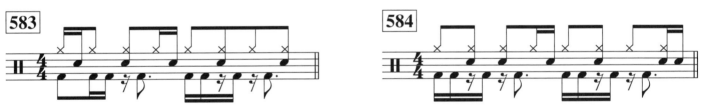

585

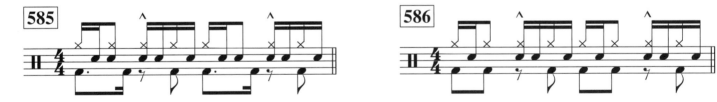

586

587

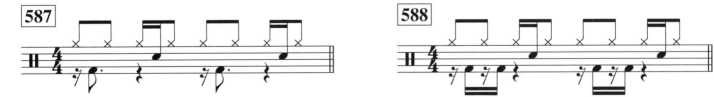

588

589

590

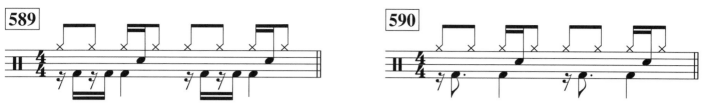

591

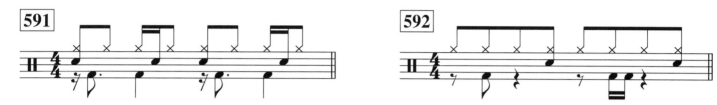

592

593

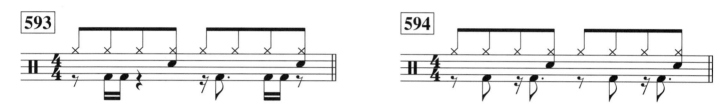

594

595

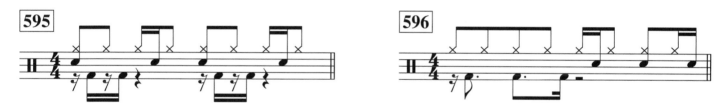

596

597

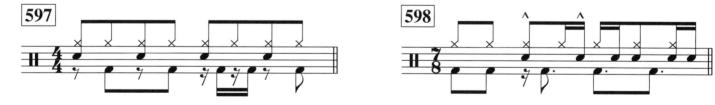

598

599

600

Solos

These solos are based on the foundation grooves mapped out in the introduction; they each start with the basic pattern and expand on it. You will notice a lot of "tricks" in the solos: displaced patterns, metric patterns that cycle over the bar line, inverted orchestrations (i.e., where the snare plays the bass figure and the bass plays the snare figure), call and response, and call and imitation. These solos will challenge you technically, rhythmically, and musically. It may help to work on each bar of a solo separately, and then put the individual measures back together. When playing the solos, think about making the rhythms flow evenly.

TRACK 01

TRACK 03

Solos *cont.*

TRACK 05

Solos *cont.*

TRACK 07

Solos *cont.*

TRACK 10

Fills

All of the fills included here are related to the primary pattern notated at the top of each page. Always keep in mind the idea and "feel" of each fill as it comes from and returns to the primary beat. Remember that musicality and the clean, technical execution of each figure are your goals.

You can also do the following to work on improving your ability to play fills. Take one of the "primary" patterns—1, 49, 97, 145, 193, 241, 289, 337, 385, 433, 481, 529—repeat it three times, and then use each subsequent pattern of the section as a fill. Since all of the patterns in each section are based on the primary (of each section), you will find that using the patterns as fills works very well. The differences among many of the beats in a particular section are often subtle—an added or subtracted note, a figure "moved" slightly, etc. —so the different patterns can often be put together to form some nice phrases. I like to use the four-bar phrase as a structure for this type of work, as it is a fairly commonplace structure in songs.

Remember that these fills are just ideas—you should also work on improvising your own! Take one of the patterns, play it three times, and then make up your own fill. Keep the four-bar phrase structure, and within that structure be creative and musical.

Fills *cont.*

TRACK 41

Play 3 times

TRACK 42

Play 3 times

TRACK 43

Play 3 times

TRACK 44

Play 3 times

TRACK 45

Play 3 times

TRACK 46

Play 3 times

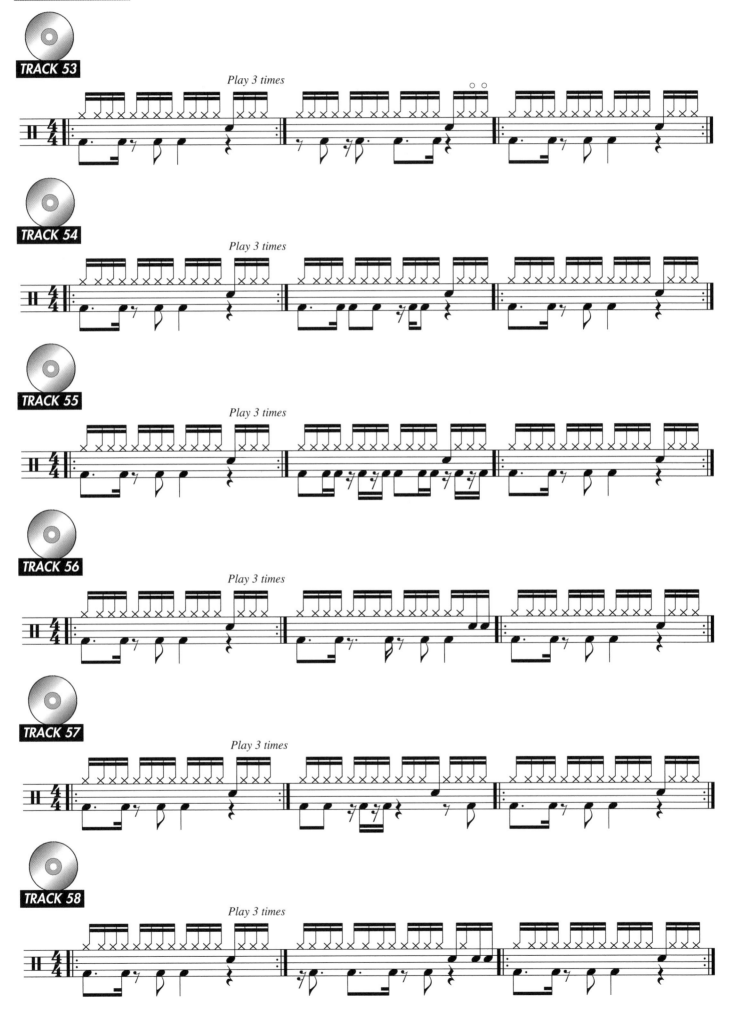

Fills *cont.*

TRACK 65

Play 3 times

TRACK 66

Play 3 times

TRACK 67

Play 3 times

TRACK 68

Play 3 times

TRACK 69

Play 3 times

TRACK 70

Play 3 times

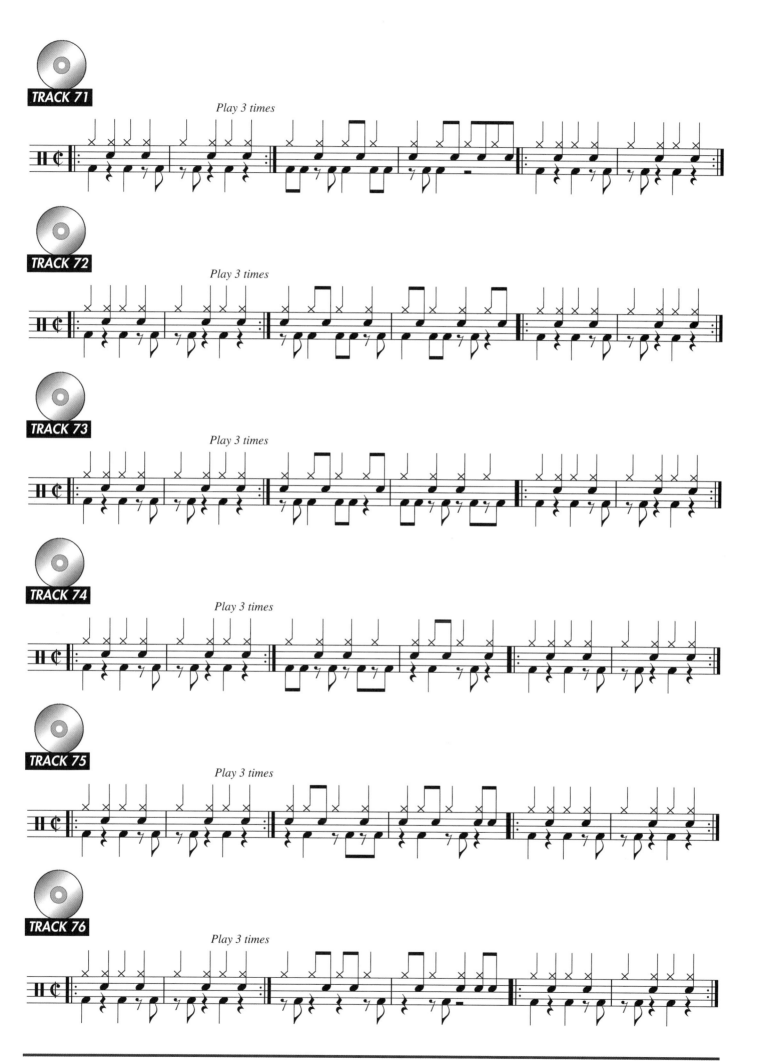

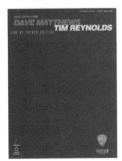
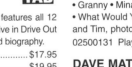